Deckchairs 4

Four short plays

Jean McConnell

Samuel French — London
www.samuelfrench-london.co.uk

DECKCHAIRS
Four short plays

Garden Pests
Grannies
Outdoor Pleasures
Remember Me

Other plays by Jean McConnell
published by Samuel French Ltd

Death is Catching (with Miles Tripp)
Deckchairs I
Deckchairs II
Deckchairs III
A Lovesome Thing
Millie's Tale

GARDEN PESTS

CHARACTERS

Helena: 50-plus
Cath: 50-plus

Scene — a secluded corner of a magnificent garden
Time — the present

A secluded corner of a magnificent garden

The garden could be implied by an open stage and birdsong. Two director's chairs stand C

The CURTAIN *rises. The Lights are bright but dim slowly as the play progresses, indicating the onset of rain*

Helena enters. She wears smart country clothes and carries a small handbag and a long umbrella, loosely folded. She moves around looking into the distance on all four sides, then moves to a chair and puts her bag on it and hooks her umbrella to its arm. She moves DS *and bends to examine a shrub (which may not be visible to us) at the front edge of the stage. She takes a notepad and pen out of her pocket and writes a note, then moves along and studies another shrub*

Cath enters. She also wears outdoor clothes but they are an odd, shabby mix. She also carries a small bag and a similar umbrella to Helena's. She puts them down by the second chair. She takes in the views around her, then joins Helena to study the same plant. She speaks with a northern accent

Cath A sport, do you think?
Helena Oh, definitely. Can't think why they've allowed it.
Cath Quite pretty in its way.
Helena They frequently are. But if it seeds …
Cath Oh, if it seeds!

They both shake their heads and suck in their breath

Helena I shall mention it on the way out.
Cath You'll do them a favour.
Helena Very foolish to leave it.
Cath Mind you, with a place this size …
Helena I would never allow it. (*Peering out front*) I think that *Passiflora caerules* down the slope is the culprit.
Cath (*following her gaze*) Oh-ho. He's the little devil all right.
Helena They'll throw their seed anywhere. Huge distances.
Cath I've known fellers like that.

Helena looks disapproving

(*Seeing Helena's look*) I beg your pardon.

Helena moves on, sees a plant and makes a note in her pad

(*Smugly*) I have that.

Helena moves on, spots another plant and makes another note

I also have that.

They move along. Cath spots a plant, brings out her notepad and pen and makes a note. Helena gives a superior smile

Helena Fairly common.

They both spot a shrub, scribble excitedly in their pads, then both put their pads away

Cath I didn't see you on the coach. (*Pause*) I said I didn't see you on ——
Helena I didn't see you either. A different coach, no doubt.
Cath That'll be it. I like to come by coach. Takes the sweat out of it. We're the Greedle Women's Guild Gardening Group. G.W.G.G.G. Sounds like a riding school, doesn't it? Maybe not.
Helena We're the King's Hibbert-under-Pegget Horticultural Society.
Cath Regular visitors to the open gardens, we are. Gives you lots of idea, we always say.
Helena Oh indeed. I've noticed several very unusual shrubs here today.
Cath You have a big garden, yourself?
Helena An acre or two. Yours?
Cath (*joking*) Ten feet of rolling parkland. No. It's a bit bigger than that. Not quite the Eden Project though. But well stocked, I'll have you know.
Helena Mine too.
Cath Well, yours, of course. No expense spared, eh?
Helena Not true at all. I maintain a true gardener seldom needs to spend a fortune on plants. A true gardener works with nature. Collecting the best seeds, layering, grafting, splitting, cross-fertilizing ... You don't need to throw money at a garden to get the best results.
Cath I agree. Especially if you haven't got any.
Helena It's a matter of principle with me. Cuttings and slips.
Cath Cuttings and slips.

Helena Friends are so kind.

Cath Mine too. Mind you, our gardens tend to look a bit samey.

Helena Oh, but you must bring something of yourself into the equation.

Cath You do get a bit knocked out when you come to a place like this. And you don't even know half the names. Right sickening. And they're down like a ton of bricks if you take the littlest leaf. I nearly got thrown out of Wisley. They emptied my holdall on to the path in front of everybody.

Helena They're very hot on holdalls.

Cath I didn't know where to put my face. Never brought a holdall since. Talking of Wisley, you know that rockery with the little pools?

Helena Oh, of course.

Cath I saw a woman take a tiny nip off a very pretty water iris. Only just then a steward hove in sight. Of course the woman fled. But it was caught in her sleeve. And the whole plant — roots and all — trailed her down the path. Laugh! (*Pause*) I've noticed there's not much grass here. I don't have grass. No room. So no lawn to worry over.

Helena I don't care for lawns. I'd sooner have flagstones and gravel.

Cath My sister in Sheffield covered their garden with decking.

Helena Decking! Ugh!

Cath Tell my sister! First winter it was all over slime. And her old man slipped and broke his leg.

Helena No more than I'd expect.

Cath It was he who wanted the decking, mind. Seen it on telly.

Helena These flash-in-the-pan fashions.

Cath Old fool.

Helena Decking. They chop down a tree in South America, saw it in planks, bring it all the way over here and lay it on the ground in Surbiton! Madness.

Cath (*sadly*) And some ancient South American tribe dies out.

Helena Yes. Well, I wouldn't go that far.

Cath Anyway, my sister's no gardener and that's a fact. Can't tell a morning glory from an evening primrose. And her red hot pokers are lukewarm at most.

Helena is not amused. She crosses L *and looks offstage. Cath follows*

There's a herbaceous border for you, eh?

Helena A heavenly drift of colour. And lots to come.

Cath Clever. What did you think of the Alpines? A tad dull, wouldn't you say?

Helena Not a bit. Subtle and understated.

Helena peers. Cath follows suit

(*Pointing*) I wonder what that violet-coloured lily is? Rather rare, I imagine. I must look it up when I get home.

Cath It's called a sacred lily. *Na-geshi-mono*. It comes from a high region of China. Needs acidic soil.

Helena You're very well informed.

Cath I read the label.

Helena Oh. (*She moves towards the chairs*)

Cath (*following*) Weren't those hostas super. In that dell. Did you see?

Helena Yes. (*Coyly*) Someone I know grows them very attractively bunched up in strange old treestumps.

Cath Oh? Who's that?

Helena It doesn't matter. Just let's say someone — rather important.

Cath Oh! You mean at Highgrove? Yes I liked that idea.

Helena Oh, you've been too. So special.

Cath You know what? I never saw a single slug. Not one. Suppose they wouldn't dare.

Helena casts her eyes to heaven and moves away. Cath glances off R

Cath (*shocked*) Heavens! That can't be a leylandii!

Helena What! No no. It's an *Abies pinsato*.

Cath Is it? Thank goodness. Gave me quite a turn.

Helena reaches her chair

Oh yes. Time for a sit down. (*She sits in the second chair*)

Helena is not best pleased but nonetheless removes her bag from her chair and sits down

Cath I'm always on the lookout for something new. Aren't you?

Helena One of my forebears was a famous plant hunter. Seeking out unusual species in farflung corners of the world.

Cath Plant hunter? Well, that's what I am, I suppose — only I don't go so far. There are some very strange plants in this garden.

Helena Indeed, yes. Known for it.

Cath Did you see that pink sort of fuchsia with orange tassels?

Helena Over by the pond with the huge Koi carp?

Cath Yes. By the pond with the huge Koi carp. The pink sort of fuchsia.

Helena With orange tassels.

Cath Yes. No idea what that is.

Helena No.
Cath Love a cutting.
Helena Yes.
Cath (*thoughtfully*) Yes.
Helena (*thoughtfully*) Yes.

Pause. Cath rummages in her bag

Cath Did you go into the conservatory?
Helena The glasshouses? Naturally.
Cath What about that gigantic "plarthritis", then, eh?
Helena Gigantic what?
Cath "Plarthritis". I love "plarthritis".
Helena Never heard of it.
Cath You know — it's those china blue florets splaying out all over.
Helena That's not "plarthritis".
Cath Well, it's something to do with aches and pains.
Helena It's certainly not called "plarthritis".
Cath What, then?
Helena Er ...
Cath It's "plarthritis", so there! And I'm going to have the last of my snack now.
Helena We stopped for luncheon at the hotel in the village.
Cath All right?
Helena Very high class.
Cath That bad, eh? I've got a tuna butty, me. (*She gets a plastic-wrapped tuna sandwich out of her handbag*) Yes. Tuna. With just a twinge of mayonnaise. Black pepper. Thinly sliced cucumber. Yummee. (*She sinks her teeth into the sandwich*)

Helena eyes the sandwich with some envy

(*Between mouthfuls*) That gardener — on the way in — with the hair — he's a bit of eye candy. Right?
Helena I really didn't notice. Tanned, naturally. Strong, by the nature of things.
Cath Quite a go-er, I'd say. They often are, don't you think? Sexy. Comes from all that propagating.
Helena (*disapprovingly*) Really.
Cath Gave me a wink as I got out of the coach. Did he give you a wink, at all?
Helena Certainly not. He handed me out in the most gentlemanly fashion.
Cath They're always kind to the elderly.

Helena He was perfectly charming. Took me into the succulent garden. To show me his special pride and joy. Quite the biggest Yucca I've ever seen.

Cath Some people have all the luck. (*She finishes her sandwich, screws up the wrapping, rises and moves around to find a rubbish bin, without success. She gets cross and makes to throw the wrapping off stage*)

Helena You must take your rubbish home.

Cath It's biodegradable.

Helena Oh, no it's not.

Cath Oh, yes it is.

Helena Oh, no it's not.

Cath Oh, all right.

Helena It's plastic.

Cath Oh shut up! (*She puts the wrapper into her bag and plumps herself down in her seat. She scowls at Helena*) That was a lovely sandwich. (*Pause*) I bet those huge Koi carp in that pond would make a delicious sandwich.

Helena Please don't be disgusting. They're perfectly beautiful. Exotic and beautiful. And they cost hundreds of pounds. Far too expensive for a sandwich.

Cath If you say so.

Helena I do say so. Because I know so. It happens that I myself had half a dozen of them in my pond. And they cost a fortune.

Cath "Had"? What happened to them? (*She is all ears*)

Helena It was a dreadful story.

Cath I can bear it.

Helena I was extremely angry. It was all the electrician's fault. No-one knows their job nowadays.

Cath Go on.

Helena You're enjoying this!

Cath Maybe. Don't know yet.

Helena It was horrible. We'd just had this beautiful pond constructed. Very elegant. With a charming fountain, a classical figure holding a dolphin — the water was to come out of its mouth, you understand.

Cath As if it was being sick.

Helena Yes. No! Just going up in a spout and then cascading down. Quite delightful.

Cath What about the Koi carp?

Helena Well — as I say — we purchased half a dozen. Some red and white. They're called Koohaku. Some light blue. They're called Asaki. Some light gold. They're called Kin-Kabuto.

Cath Never mind all that.

Helena They're Japanese, you understand.

Cath I know! So what?

Helena So we put them in the pond. And they were all swimming around perfectly happily. But that stupid man who'd put in the fountain had wired it up all wrong. And when we switched it on, the Koi carp all leapt up in the air and fell back dead.

Cath By heck.

Helena It was a terrible shock for us.

Cath Not much fun for the fish either. Well, I'd never have any drama like that. A few shubunkins were the most excitement we ever had. But, of course, there was the saga of the snails in the mailbox.

Pause. Cath rummages in her bag and finds a sweet which she unwraps slowly. Despite herself, Helena is waiting to hear the saga

Helena Well?

Cath Well what?

Helena Well, what about the snails?

Cath Oh those. Oh yes. Ha! Funny. You want to hear?

Helena You have aroused my curiosity.

Cath Right. Well ... There's a little mailbox set in a wall outside my house, see? Anyroad, I got the idea that snails were getting inside and chewing up the letters. Because there were all these slimy trails all over the place. I told the a postman but he wouldn't believe me. Anyway I proved it. You know how?

Helena No.

Cath I posted myself a letter. And sure enough it was delivered next day chewed right round the edges and all over snailtrail. I stuck up a notice beside the mailbox warning people not to put their post in it.

Helena Very wise.

Cath And would you know, next day my little notice was chewed right round the edges and all over snailtrail!

Helena Good heavens.

Cath (*giggling*) You get this picture, don't you? All the female snails munching at the pale pink love letters and getting silly ideas. And all the old male snails chomping on the bitter brown envelopes, saying they're an acquired taste — and ——

Helena Yes, yes, yes. But what happened in the end?

Cath I waylaid the postman and insisted he explored the box thoroughly. And do you know there were twenty-five snails living in that mailbox. Yes. Twenty-five snails living in a mailbox. Sounds like a comic song.

Helena I don't know that they warrant a song. Snails are the gardener's greatest enemy, in my estimation.

Cath I'm with you there. And will they climb! Every mountain, till they reach their goal...which is usually your favourite plant.

Helena Destruction personified. I lost my most treasured clematis to them last year. A Paternoster glandulosa. Not on the general market.

Cath They've got one here, did you see?

Helena Yes, I noticed. Over in the Japanese garden.

Cath In the Japanese garden. Yes.

Helena Yes.

Pause

The dahlias are rather early. (*She pronounces it "darlias"*)

Cath Oh here we go. They're "daylias"! "Daylias!"

Helena "Darlias", if you don't mind.

Cath Since when? They've always been "daylias".

Helena Depends where you come from, I suppose.

Cath Don't you come the old acid with me, lady.

Helena Wouldn't dream of it. You're a "daylia" person. I'm a "darlia" person. I'll go on growing "darlias". You go on growing "daylias".

Cath No, I won't. I hate the things.

Helena There you are then.

Cath I suppose you're one of those who call a begonia a bergenia.

Helena Good grief! They're completely different! A bergenia's a foliage plant. Sometimes called elephant's ears. Or then again sometimes called St Patrick's cabbage and ——

Cath Will you give over! You're doing my head in. Anyway, I don't grow vegetables.

Helena I think we're getting our wires crossed. (*She turns her back on Cath*)

Cath It's because I didn't give you a tuna sandwich, isn't it? Admit it! Admit it!

Helena suddenly cries out in pain. She clutches her hand

What is it? What is it?

Helena I've been stung by a wasp! Ooooh!

Cath Hold on! I've got some stuff for it. Hold on.

Cath rummages in her handbag and produces a tube of cream. She applies it to Helena's hand

Here it is. There you are. Never travel without it.

Helena Oh, thank you. How very resourceful.

Cath There must be a nest nearby.

Helena I shall report it on the way out. That's very kind of you. It feels better already. Just one of the hazards of horticulture.

Cath Just one of the hazards. Nevertheless ...

Helena Nevertheless ...

They both sigh agreeably. Cath returns the tube to her bag

Cath I wouldn't be without my garden. I just love it.

Helena One does.

Cath However small. Just the feel of the earth. And its smell. And after the rain in February when you go out and there's some bulb suddenly reared its little head. Bless its heart. Just when you need it.

Helena Yes. I can't imagine giving up my garden either. (*Thoughtfully*) Though maybe less beds ... Increase the shrubbery ...

Cath When you're old, I suppose, then you're compelled to leave.

Helena It doesn't bear contemplating.

Cath It happened to my aunt. She was going into a home but she made a terrible fuss about leaving her garden. She was always a mad keen gardener. The last day she stood at the gate, clinging on to it. Screaming. We couldn't prise her loose from it. Neighbours came out trying to reason with her. You know, saying "You'll have a nice garden at the home and no work to do" and all that guff. She just howled on like a child having to part with an old teddy they were going to burn. You know.

Helena No, I don't.

Cath Well, I do. Anyway, she was just crying out and shrieking like a mad thing.

Helena How frightful. Did your aunt accept it and give up in the end?

Cath Well, no. She went on screaming at us and we went on pulling at her. Then she fainted clean away.

Helena Oh poor soul.

Cath Yes. (*Pause*) Turned out she had her finger caught in the latch.

Helena frowns. She is not sure whether she has been taken in. Pause. She scans the sky

Helena I thought I felt a spot of rain.

Cath You're right. Clouds are gathering. Still it's been a grand afternoon. Reckon I've seen most everything.

Helena I believe I've done very well.

Cath Me too. Done very well. But admit it, you didn't see that "plarthritis".

Helena There is no such thing as a "plarthritis"! It's called a ... Oh, I can't think. How tiresome.

Cath I may not know all the Latin names but I know my plants. (*Pause*)

I said, I know my plants.

Helena I heard you. I just don't think boastfulness is a very attractive character trait. I do pride myself on not being opinionated.

Cath All I'm saying is I have a keen eye. It's a fact. That's not boasting.

Helena What? Huh! You're a regular Baobab tree!

Cath What do you mean by that?

Helena Oh. Do you not know the legend of the Baobab? I heard it in Africa when we were on safari.

Cath Oh where else!

Helena Well, the Baobab was once the most beautiful tree in the forest. Now it is probably the ugliest. Shall I tell you why?

Cath Do I have a choice?

Helena The Baobab tree suffered from the sin of pride, you see. And one day God leaned down and told it to stop all that boasting or it would come to grief. But the Baobab went on preening itself and showing off. So God stooped down and plucked it out of the earth and turned it upside down and thrust it back in headfirst. And that is why the Baobab has all its flowers hidden underground and its roots sticking up in the air. Not a pretty sight.

Pause

Cath What a load of rubbish.

Helena I think its charming.

Cath I think it's raining.

Helena Better get back to the coaches.

The sound of rain begins

The two women bring rainwear out of their bags. Helena's is stylish. Cath's is a white plastic coverall. Helena shakes hers out and dons it. Cath struggles into hers

So useful, this.

Cath So's mine.

Helena Folds down to nothing.

Cath So does mine.

Helena And not unattractive.

Cath My husband says mine looks like a condom.

Helena Pardon?

Cath A condom. (*Chuckling naughtily*) My husband says ——

Helena Enough! Please! If you don't mind!

The sound of rain gets heavier. Thunder is heard

Cath Oh dear. It's coming on fast!
Helena Where's my umbrella?

The two women dive for their umbrellas. Both of them pick up the wrong one

Cath Hang about — that's mine!
Helena Oh, any brolly in a storm!

Helena puts up Cath's umbrella. Out falls a shower of cuttings

Helena Cuttings ! That's what you've been up to! It's your sort get garden visitors a bad name! (*She goes to take her own umbrella from Cath*)

Cath draws back

Cath Hold on, lady! Let's see what *you've* been up to! (*She opens Helena's umbrella*)

An even larger shower of cuttings falls out of Helena's umbrella

Ha! Mrs High-and-Mighty! What do you say about *that*!
Helena There's only one thing to say. We just need more umbrellas!

The two women exchange umbrellas, grab their bags and rush towards the exit, Helena leading the way

The storm increases as —

— *the* Curtain *falls*

GRANNIES

CHARACTERS

Barbara: 40/50
Jenny: 40/50

Scene — A secluded part of the seafront at a flourishing resort
Time — the present

A secluded part of the seafront at a flourishing resort

Two municipal canvas chairs are set C

The CURTAIN *rises. The Lights are bright. Jenny is sitting in the chair* R. *She is an attractive woman wearing casual clothes, her hair natural rather than styled. She is reading a crime novel. Beside her is a baby's pram, the modern carrycot type, facing* US *with the hood up; the occupant is silent and invisible to the audience. Jenny's foot is poised on the pram wheel, ready to jiggle if necessary*

Barbara approaches from L. *She is well-dressed, elegant even. She is wheeling a carriage-built pram with the hood up, its occupant also invisible and silent. She pauses when she sees Jenny, then moves to the chair* L *and sets her pram beside it, facing* US

Barbara (*rocking her pram and speaking down into it*) There, there, little one. Settle down to a nice sleep. Yes, yes, that's right, sweetheart.

Barbara puts the brake on and sits in the chair L. *She looks at Jenny. Jenny, becoming aware of her gaze, looks up, nods pleasantly, then returns to her book*

Pause

Teething.
Jenny (*looking up*) What? Oh dear, I sympathize. (*Smiling wryly*) Me, I thought I'd seen the last of all that. But no. (*She goes back to her book*)

Pause

Barbara Lovely day to bring the baby out. To get the sea air. Does them good.
Jenny Makes them sleep. That's a bonus. (*She turns a page*)
Barbara Oh. Yes. (*Pause*) Your grandchild?
Jenny Yes. Sammy.

Barbara Sammy?

Jenny Yes.

Barbara My grandchild too. She's such a good little thing. She was a bit underweight at birth. But she's put it on and now she's quite plump. (*Pause*) With such a beautiful skin. They do have such lovely skin, don't they? (*Pause*) Her hair was quite black at first but it's going almost blonde now.

Jenny (*reluctantly lowering her book*) What's her name?

Barbara What?

Jenny Her name?

Barbara (*after a tiny pause*) Melisande.

Jenny Meli ... ? (*She stifles a giggle*) Ah. Don't get many of those.

Barbara Of what?

Jenny You don't get many Melisandes.

Barbara Don't you? It's pretty.

Jenny Oh yes, oh yes. Old-fashioned and very sweet.

Jenny tries to return to her book, but Barbara turns towards her, clearly wanting an in-depth conversation. Jenny closes her book and listens

Barbara It's wonderful — getting the chance to have the baby to look after. That's the trouble when your children live abroad. You see them so infrequently. And they grow up so quickly. I've missed so much.

Jenny I have Sammy all day.

Barbara All day. That must be such a joy for you.

Jenny (*after a tiny pause*) He's a darling, yes. A sweetie.

Barbara Do his parents pick him up when they get home from work?

Jenny No. It's not quite like that.

Barbara Oh.

Jenny There isn't a father ...

Barbara I understand.

Jenny Well, not around.

Barbara Ah. He's your daughter's baby though.

Jenny Oh, yes.

Barbara And she picks him up from work.

Jenny No. She picks him up from school.

Barbara I don't follow.

Jenny My daughter is a schoolgirl.

Barbara I see. Well, I don't see actually.

Jenny It was — well — a mistake.

Barbara Oh dear.

Jenny The boy was very young too. But Emma was sure he'd stick by her. All very romantic. I wish they wouldn't always do *Romeo and Juliet* at school! The boy's parents put an end to that, of course. As soon as they knew about it. I don't blame them. He was a bright lad. Had a good future ahead of him. No point wrecking his life. Hampered by a baby so soon.

Barbara But your daughter …

Jenny She's bright too. I think she'll do well.

Barbara But isn't she "hampered" as you rather oddly put it?

Jenny Not so's you'd notice. I mean, she's put Sammy over to me.

Barbara Oh, but that's good!

Jenny My daughter's going away to college soon.

Barbara But that's splendid. You'll have the little one all to yourself.

Jenny I've had four, you know.

Barbara Four? Four what?

Jenny I've brought up four children already. Emma is the youngest.

Barbara Ah.

Jenny The novelty wears off.

Barbara You do put things strangely. Surely it's wonderful to have another in the nest again. Isn't it? May I look at Sammy?

Jenny If you like.

Barbara leans across and peers into Jenny's pram

Barbara He's beautiful.

Jenny Yes. He is.

Barbara So's mine. But I'd rather you didn't disturb her. She's sleeping so soundly.

Jenny (*who hadn't intended to*) That's all right.

Barbara You're so fortunate. Four babies.

Jenny Two were twins.

Barbara Identical?

Jenny Yes. Except in character. Daisy's serious. But Josie was a right tearaway. They've all moved off now. Got their own places. Married …

Barbara But now you've got a fifth! Lucky. So lucky.

Jenny It's a lot of work. The energy needed. You forget.

Barbara You don't mind though, I'll be bound.

Jenny I just thought I'd seen the last of it.

Barbara But it's a labour of love, isn't it? I only wish I'd had more time with this little one. But when the family are moving here, there and everywhere.

Jenny Is your son-in-law in the Services?

Barbara I beg pardon?

Jenny In the Forces? Diplomatic Corp? Is that why they get moved around?

Barbara Oh, yes. Yes, that's it. I see them so seldom.

Jenny That's a shame.

Barbara I do miss my grandchild. This is only the second time I've seen her. And I expect they'll be whisking her away, to the other side of the world. I don't know when I'll see her again after that.

Jenny Perhaps you could visit them.

Barbara Perhaps I could. But it's not the same is it?

Jenny The same as what?

Barbara No, it's not the same.

Jenny Think positively. Maybe later on, you could take the child away for a little holiday. What about that?

Barbara Oh wouldn't that be a marvellous idea! Wouldn't it be grand. To have her all to myself. But I don't think they'd let me.

Jenny You never know. In time, your daughter might be glad of the break.

Barbara Oh no. She is such a devoted mother. She hardly ever lets her out of her sight.

Jenny Well, you've got her today, haven't you.

Barbara Yes. (*Pause*) That's because my daughter had to go to the hospital.

Jenny Hospital? Nothing serious, I hope?

Barbara No, no. Just a routine check-up. She'll be home this evening. Like your Emma. But she'll take the baby off with her. Unlike your Emma. (*She sighs*) I envy you so much.

Jenny You do?

There is a long pause. Jenny sits very still, a memory surfacing

I cried for a month.

Barbara You cried? For Emma?

Jenny No. For me.

Barbara Cried.

Jenny With disappointment. I'd just been accepted into the Open University. And Ed and I were planning a really long holiday first. We'd never been able to kick up much over the years. Not with four kids. No money enough either really. Not that we'd minded. We enjoyed our children.

Barbara Naturally.

Jenny Why "naturally"? Not everyone does.

Barbara Oh, you can't genuinely believe that.

Jenny I honestly don't know why some people have children. They go

out to work all the time and let other people bring them up. So why
have them at all? It's not compulsory.

Barbara (*confused*) Compulsory?

Jenny No, we had all the best years of ours, watching them develop and
change. Every day. Every hour sometimes, it seemed to me. Who'd
want to miss it? But you're glad when they've grown up.

Barbara You said you cried?

Jenny When you're free at last — I mean of scrimping and saving and
the responsibilities ... Emma looked set fair to get to college and be the
real brains of the family. Have an important career. Then she comes
home with this bombshell. It wasn't too late at that point to have it
aborted.

Barbara On no! What a terrible thought!

Jenny Terrible? It might not have been that terrible. She was just a child
herself, wasn't she? She had no idea of what it entails. A baby. Well,
you know, don't you?

Barbara Yes, yes, of course.

Jenny Getting up in the night ... Heart jumping when it got sick.
Keeping it warm in winter and cool in summer. Cleaning it up at one
end or the other. And guiding it, as best you can, for the next fourteen
years. Trying to make a decent person out of the crumpled little scrap
that you've thrust out into this harsh world. I've done it four times.
And made a lot of pig's ears, I bet. But I got it right sometimes too no
question. (*Pause*) Still I cried.

Barbara But even so ...

Jenny Emma was the last of my babies, so I thought. I tried to make her
understand. She wasn't like those poor girls from unloving families
who need to have something in their lives that's theirs alone, to give
them back some love they've never had. That wasn't Emma. She'd
always been surrounded with affection. Always.

Barbara Oh, I'm sure.

Jenny She thought the boy would stay with her. He was only sixteen.
He made her believe it. I think he believed it himself. He wasn't a bad
boy at all. Thought they'd marry. Imagine it. His parents moved away
and took him with them. He's going to University. Emma was cut up
about that. It was all too late. Too late. Sammy was born. And we all
adore him. But he's more mine than Emma's.

Barbara I still think it's lovely.

Jenny All right. But we had to let our dream go. Ed and me. No more
world cruise. No more serious fell-walking. No more taking a pub
together. All silly dreams. And not necessary. But sometimes I think
it's a life for a life. And it's not Emma's life. She's hardly felt the
difference. Takes part in all the school activities. Goes on trips. Goes
out dancing.

Barbara You sounded quite bitter then.

Jenny I did. How surprising.

Barbara He's worth it though.

Jenny I just wish it hadn't been a case of either/or. The choice wasn't fair. Wasn't a choice at all actually.

Barbara Of course not. And Sammy has probably done better having you. Think of what some of these teenage mothers get up to. And your husband's made the best of it in the end, hasn't he?

Jenny He took the Emma business very badly. She was his little dabchick. He seemed bewildered. Then he shouted at her. It was terrible. I'd never heard him do that. Ever. At a certain point there wasn't anything to do but go on. But sometimes I see an expression on his face ... He's a good man. But sometimes I think I'm asking too much of him. To stay with me even. A weary grandmother, rather than a funtime partner. Dancing into the sunset. Poor Ed. I hope he loves me enough. Sometimes I wonder ... (*Pause*) He's turned to golf.

Barbara He's turned to God?

Jenny Golf! Golf!

Barbara Sorry. That's quite different

Jenny (*after a pause; wryly*) Yes. Well, I think so.(*She looks into the pram*) Well, Sammy is here. And we're stuck with him. (*With deep affection*) And he's the cutest little sausage in the world.

Barbara They're all so special in their different ways. (*Clucking gently into her pram*) Giddy giddy giddy.

Jenny That's true. (*She half-rises and leans towards Barbara's pram*)

Barbara (*fending Jenny away*) No, no. Don't disturb him.

Jenny (*surprised*) I thought you said it was a girl.

Barbara No, it's a boy. I said a boy.

Jenny No, you didn't. Melisande, you said.

Barbara Oh. Oh, silly me. I was thinking of my godchild. Fancy getting them muddled. No, this is a little boy.

Jenny He's wearing a pink bonnet.

Barbara It's sunny.

Jenny Not very.

Jenny, looking a bit puzzled, sits back in her chair

Barbara I'm surprised at you. I'd have thought you were so experienced with small children. You surely know how vulnerable their heads are.

Jenny I agree, but ——

Barbara When I see the way some of these young mothers dress their babies. No woolly hat even in the coldest weather. And their little feet bare — quite blue sometimes. Next day they'll be banging on the doctor's door with a sick infant. And all cramped up in some miniscule buggy — all set for curvature of the spine later in life. And endlessly sucking on sugar drinks — ruining their teeth and their appetite. What's wrong with clean water when they're thirsty?

Jenny (*joking*) Better than dirty, I suppose.

Barbara (*crossly*) I'm being serious.

Jenny (*trying to lighten things*) You really are a worry-guts.

Barbara Do you think so? I just love them so much. I love their little hands — the way they'll cling on to your finger. It's their first instinct, you know. To hold on to security. The fear of falling. Those little fingernails. Like tiny pearly seashells. You find them on the beach.

Jenny Fingernails?

Barbara Seashells. The size of a baby's fingernails. Darwin had it right, you know.

Jenny You've lost me now.

Barbara The origin of the species. How we all relate. Way back. How we came out of the sea.

Jenny (*teasing*) I thought that was Venus. She came out of a seashell. On the coast of Cyprus.

Barbara (*earnestly*) What do you mean? I don't follow.

Jenny (*giving up*) Nor do I!

Pause. Jenny flicks at her book

Barbara No. We're talking about the Coelacanth.

Jenny Are we? Please don't let's. Look, do you mind if I go on reading, I've just got to the good bit.

Barbara The nub. (*Looking at the title*) Lightweight stuff.

Jenny I can't read heavy stuff ——

Barbara (*patronizingly*) I understand.

Jenny — because I haven't the time right now. I thought I'd explained.

Barbara Sorry.

Pause. Jenny reads. Barbara rocks her pram

The young fathers are just as bad. (*Pause*) All covered in studs and rings and leather bits. (*Pause*) Think they're so clever, with the baby dangling down their front. (*Pause*) Paying it no heed whatever.

Jenny (*riled herself now*) You know you really shouldn't!

Barbara What?

Jenny Judge a sausage by its skin. I saw a young chap only today like that. Like you say, all tattoos and puce hair with a tiny baby dangling

on him. And, all right, like you, I felt a bit anxious. And then I saw
him kiss the baby on the top of its head. So tenderly. We shouldn't be
too quick to judge.

Barbara They leave their prams outside Mothercare. "Mother-care".
Huh!

Jenny They take the babies inside! You really mustn't assume ——

Barbara Not always! And those pushchairs, facing out to the traffic
— who invented those, may I ask? The poor child must be terrified.
Thrust out into the road under a lorry. And breathing all those fumes.
A baby should be able to see its mother. To sit facing her. To give it
confidence. To know its mother loves it and wants to see it face to
face. Enjoys watching it. But I suppose so few of them do. At least in
Romania they're honest ...

Jenny What are you talking about ... ?

Barbara (*very agitated by now*)They just shove them in an orphanage!
They don't pretend they want them!

*Jenny looks at Barbara anxiously. She peers across again at Barbara's
pram*

Jenny He's very still.

Barbara What?

Jenny Your — little one.

Barbara He's sleeping. I said. Small children must have lots of sleep.
The minute they start making a fuss you put them to bed for a while
because they're usually overtired. No need to smack them. Just put
them to bed to rest.

Jenny Well, yes — I agree. But they're not all exactly the same...

Barbara They need to know the boundaries. Their limits. That someone
cares enough to make rules to keep them safe.

Jenny You're right, of course. (*But she is having some doubts about
Barbara*) Are you sure your baby is OK?

Barbara Oh yes. He's been sleeping all the afternoon. Ever since I
brought him down to the seafront.

Jenny Where from?

Barbara Where from? Where from?

Jenny (*suddenly worried*) Where did you get that baby.

Barbara What do you mean?

Jenny What I said. Where did you get that baby?

Barbara I told you. He's mine.

Jenny You mean he's your daughter's.

Barbara No. He's mine.

Jenny Yours?

Barbara For the time being, of course. Just for the time being. Unfortunately. (*She listens keenly to the following, nodding*)

Jenny Yes. I see. Look, you mustn't let it get to you too much, you know. I mean your grandchild going abroad. You can send her — him lots of cards. Little gifts. Keep in close touch — until you see him again. Perhaps it won't be too long. Maybe sooner than you expect.

Pause

Barbara I tell you what. I have an idea. Perhaps sometime I could take your Sammy out. Give you a bit of time to yourself.

Jenny I don't think so.

Barbara Give you time to study. Your Foundation Course? The Open University, you said.

Jenny (*ruefully*) There is that.

Barbara I could manage a whole day if you like. Where do you live?

Jenny (*looking curiously at Barbara*) But I don't think so. No.

Pause. Barbara looks lost. She begins to rock her pram rhythmically. Jenny watches her. She is really troubled now

(*Very gently*) You know, I've heard that some women can get such a deep longing for a baby that they get quite — carried away. I've heard they've even been known to — borrow them.

Barbara (*vaguely*) Borrow a baby.

Jenny Just for a little while. They usually take them back. And no harm done.

Barbara Of course. No harm done.

Pause

Jenny But the mothers can get frantic, naturally.

Barbara Well, they shouldn't have left them unattended in the first place, should they?

Jenny No, I agree. But they don't imagine anyone will do such a thing. (*Pause*) After all, the police regard it very seriously if anyone takes away a baby.

Barbara The police?

Jenny Yes.

Barbara Are you going to call the police?

Jenny I didn't say that.

Barbara Why would you call the police?

Jenny Because — if your baby's not well, maybe we should get help.

Barbara What are you talking about?
Jenny Just let me look at her — him.
Barbara He's a boy. I said he's a boy! I believe you think I stole him.
  How could you think that! It's mine! It's mine. Go away! Go away
  from me!

*Jenny rises and quickly crosses behind Barbara and looks into her pram.
She bends close and picks up the baby, which is wrapped in a shawl*

  (*Getting very distressed*) Stop it! Stop it! How dare you!

*They struggle, Barbara clutching the shawl, Jenny holding on to the
baby. Finally the shawl falls off. Jenny gasps. The "baby" is a quite
lifelike doll. She holds it up, amazed, and stares at Barbara*

Jenny It's a doll! It's just a doll.

Barbara seizes the doll away from Jenny and cradles it in her arms

Barbara That's right. My doll. Mine. Mine.

*Barbara wraps the doll tenderly in the shawl. She faces Jenny, wild-
eyed, defensive, rocking the doll in her arms*

Jenny A doll.
Barbara So?

There is a long pause

Jenny (*softly*) There's never been a baby?

There is a long pause. Barbara stops rocking

Barbara There's — never — been — a — baby.

*Barbara puts the doll carefully back in the pram and sits beside it staring
out in front. Jenny crosses, kneels beside Barbara and takes her hand,
patting it kindly*

Jenny (*at last*) Didn't your daughter have a baby at all?
Barbara (*turning to Jenny*) What?
Jenny Your daughter ...
Barbara (*dreamily*) I never had a daughter. I never had a child at all.

(*She giggles*) And me with my child-bearing hips, my dear! (*Pause. Tears start to come*) But no baby. Never a baby. Never ever. Too late now. Time's up. Well and truly. (*She dries her eyes*) Excuse me.

Barbara rises. She pushes Jenny gently aside, then moves round behind the pram and takes the handle. Without another look at Jenny, she pushes the pram slowly off R

Jenny watches her go, looking after her with compassion. Then she slowly moves to her own pram and sits looking into it. She lays a protective arm across it, as ——

— *the* CURTAIN *falls*

OUTDOOR PLEASURES

CHARACTERS

Deirdre: 40/50
Auntie Tottie: 60-plus

Scene — a section of the large gardens of a country estate
Time — the present

A section of the large gardens of a country estate

The CURTAIN *rises. The Lights suggest an early evening in summer*

Deirdre enters R. *She is aged between forty and fifty and is from the
Home Counties. She is wearing trousers and a jumper and an anorak.
She is carrying two director's chairs and a picnic basket and has a rug
over her shoulder. Right now she is a little stressed. She staggers* C

Deirdre (*brightly*) Now, here's a good place, Auntie. Shall we settle
here? (*She puts down the chairs then spreads the rug on the ground
and puts the basket on it*) We'll have a good view of the play from
here, don't you think, Auntie? (*She sets up the chairs side by side to
face the front*) I believe I sat here once before. Could see very well.
Auntie? (*Looking around*) Auntie? (*She moves* R *and looks off stage*)
Auntie! Where have you got to?

Auntie Tottie enters L. *She is a shrewd Northerner. Like Deirdre she is
wearing clothes suitable for a bitter English summer evening. She is
leaning on an umbrella. She gives a groan*

(*Turning*) Auntie ! I told you to follow me!
Tottie I walked through some nettles.
Deirdre You couldn't have. There aren't any.
Tottie Not the way you came, maybe. The way I came there were
nettles.
Deirdre Well, you should have followed me! Not go wandering away.
Tottie You took off like a whippet.
Deirdre With all this gear? I did no such thing. Anyway, we'll set
ourselves down here. All right? (*She takes off her anorak and busies
herself*)
Tottie Will we be able to see from here?
Deirdre Yes we will. (*Gesturing out front*) All this is where the actors
will be performing. We're in the front row, Auntie. That was the idea
of coming early.
Tottie What if someone puts their chairs down in front of us?
Deirdre They won't. They're very nice here. Everyone who comes to
see open-air Shakespeare is nice.
Tottie But suppose they do put their chairs down in ——

Deirdre They *won't*!

Tottie You've a touching faith in human nature.

Deirdre Auntie — they buy their tickets to support charity. They bring their own seats. They bring their own picnic. They bring their own rugs for the second half. They bring their own raincoats and umbrellas. They bring champagne. They are a nice class of person.

Tottie If you say so. (*She sits in the chair* L)

Deirdre A lot of them are my personal friends. From bridge, you know.

Tottie I play bridge.

Deirdre Do you, Auntie? You used not to.

Tottie I'm taking a course. We could play with your friends.

Deirdre (*hastily*) We don't play so much in the summer. Get out. In the garden. Go to outdoor Shakespeare! Anyway, there won't be much time.

Tottie It was kind of you to ask me down for the weekend.

Deirdre Not at all.

Tottie You didn't think I'd accept, did you? You looked quite white when I said "Yes, thank you: when?"

Deirdre Oh Auntie, how droll of you. We were delighted you said you'd come. Not seen you for so many years. It was a pity we should meet again in such sad circumstances.

Pause. Deirdre kneels and gets the picnic out during the following

Tottie He'd had a fair innings.

Deirdre Oh, he had. And a great old life.

Tottie No shortage of brass there. I hope he remembered you.

Deirdre Remembered ... ? Oh, you mean in his will. Well, I don't know ...

Tottie He did me. But then so he should.

Deirdre It was a very fine funeral.

Tottie He left a tidy sum for the catering. The place was awash with booze.

Deirdre It certainly was.

Tottie Your Robert was pretty well legless at the end.

Deirdre Robert was? I don't recall.

Tottie Quite. It was at the end that you both flung out the invitation to me.

Deirdre Now Auntie, we meant it. We're pleased you made the journey all this way. I hope you're having a good time. Your bed's comfy, isn't it? And I think you're really going to enjoy this evening.

Pause

Tottie Why didn't Robert come?

Deirdre I told you, Auntie. Robert's off on a golf match. He simply couldn't get out of it, try as he may. He'll be back tomorrow — evening.

Tottie gives Deirdre a look

Now then, let's have our picnic. Guess what? We've got champagne! It's from Robert. You see? (*She flourishes a bottle of champagne from the basket*)

Tottie Does he know something we don't?

Deirdre Oh, you are a terror! (*She sets to work to open the bottle*)

Tottie What are we seeing anyway?

Deirdre (*struggling*) I told you. Get the glasses out, will you?

Tottie I've forgotten.

Deirdre In the basket.

Tottie No, the play.

Deirdre There's a leaflet.

Tottie Where?

Deirdre In the *basket*!

Tottie All right all right! (*Crossly*) Lot of fuss about nowt (*She searches in the basket*)

Deirdre Nearly right. *Much Ado About Nothing.*

Tottie What ? (*Producing a leaflet*) Oh yes. *Much Ado About Nothing.* (*Sarcastically*) Catchy title.

Deirdre (*still wrestling with the bottle*) I'm sure he knew his audience.

Tottie I think I saw an actor over there. Shall I get him to help you.

Deirdre No, no. He's preparing for his part. Don't disturb him.

Tottie He was drinking a pint of beer.

Deirdre So ...?

Tottie Nobody seems to be in a hurry.

Deirdre They may be worrying about the weather. It is a bit overcast.

Tottie Won't they act it just the same? We brought an umbrella.

Deirdre They'll play if it just spits and spots or drizzles. They go on, despite getting quite soaking sometimes. Very brave. But not if it pours, of course. Nobody enjoys themselves if it pours. (*Jokily*) If wet, in Scout hut! (*She laughs merrily*)

Tottie doesn't

You haven't been to enough of these, Auntie. I don't suppose you've been to any, actually, have you?

Tottie Yes, I have.

Deirdre You've been to an open-air theatre?

Tottie Yes, I have.

Deirdre Where?

Tottie Oberammergau.

Deirdre (*deeply jealous*) You never did, Auntie. I doubt if you can spell it.

Tottie I went with the over-sixties. In a coach.

Deirdre Did you enjoy it?

Tottie Very much. Plenty of room. Ample onboard facilities. But loads of comfort stops too. And we had a grand singsong all the way back.

Deirdre What about the music?

Tottie Oh, my friend Wag had this concertina. He's a right whizz on the concertina.

Deirdre fears her leg is being pulled. She abandons the bottle and, during the following, offers the box of sandwiches and a carton of juice to Tottie and sits in the chair R

Deirdre Fine. Well, let's have a sandwich. Smoked salmon. No expense spared! Would you like some orange juice? I'll have another go at the champagne later.

Tottie takes a sandwich and the carton of juice. They eat and drink during the following

The place to go to is the Globe, of course. So wonderful. After nearly five hundred years. Have you been to the Globe?

Tottie Don't think so. What's on there? *Mousetrap* still?

Deirdre No Auntie, *The Mousetrap* is in the West End. The Globe Theatre is the place they built on the South Bank, based entirely on the original Elizabethan one.

Tottie Oh yes. Why did they do that?

Deirdre It's so that people can experience Shakespeare's plays just as they were presented in Shakespeare's own day. There aren't masses of stage lamps, see? Just the natural daylight. Mind you, the sun shines full in the audience's eyes instead of on the actors. But maybe it did in those days too. And then there's a place for people to stand and watch if they can't afford a seat. Just like in those days. I'm not quite sure why they don't provide stools or something actually. But people seem to like to mill about. And some of them stay right through to the end. If you do have a seat on the benches, you can hire a sort of cardboard corset so that your back doesn't give out. It works very

well. Everybody snuggles up together. It's very friendly. And if you've
missed a bit of dialogue — and you sometimes do when the actors turn
their heads aside — a Japanese will tell you what they said. They
always bring the script.

Tottie This is a very nice picnic, Deirdre.

Deirdre Thank you, Auntie. I bought you a synopsis of *Much Ado*. Did
you take look at it?

Tottie A bit. That Beatrice and Benedick reminded me of the couple in
Kiss Me Kate the way they carry on. Bit of a crib really.

Deirdre Well he's allowed to crib. He wrote them both. It's *The Taming
of the Shrew*, Auntie. You know ...

Tottie No harm in a bit of re-cycling, I suppose. That woman we passed
round the back of the bushes, did you say she was playing the leading
lady?

Deirdre Beatrice. That's right.

Tottie And her son's playing the hero.

Deirdre Of course not. Hero is the name of the young girl whose story
is the main part of the plot. That man with the green costume ——

Tottie With the beer?

Deirdre Benedick, that's right ...

Tottie Looks young enough to be her grandson!

Deirdre Lower your voice, Auntie. Casting these parts is sometimes
quite difficult. (*Loudly*) Don't you think all the trees and bushes make
a lovely setting for it?

Tottie Don't know yet. Haven't seen the play.

Deirdre You will when it starts, won't you. Just imagine. It's such a
pretty place. Perfect for *A Midsummer Night's Dream*.

Tottie Are we seeing *A Midsummer Night's Dream*? You didn't say we
were seeing *A Midsummer Night's Dream* ...

Deirdre No, no, no!

Tottie Now I did see *that* once.

Deirdre You didn't.

Tottie I did! It had a man in it was supposed to be donkey.

Deirdre It doesn't only have that.

Tottie That's the bit I saw. On the telly. There was this girl who fancied
him. Bit iffy, I thought.

Deirdre You should have watched the rest of it.

Tottie Got near the knuckle did it?

Deirdre No! All I was about to say was that they did it here last year.
And it was so charming with the characters popping in and out of the
bushes. The director made very good use of them.

Tottie I think I'd like to do the same.

Deirdre What?

Tottie Make use of the bushes.

Deirdre There was a Portaloo over by the entrance.

Tottie Oh, I hate those. I always think they'll fall over.

Deirdre But it's going to start any minute.

Tottie No, it isn't. I felt a spot of rain. Why couldn't they hold this play in a theatre?

Deirdre Because it wouldn't be open-air Shakespeare then, would it? Everybody understands about open-air productions in the English summer. The uncertainty is part of the fun.

Tottie I'll go in the interval.

Deirdre That's the idea. Have a sausage roll. Oh, I believe the actors are coming!

Tottie Are we going to be able to hear anything with the birds and the wind and the aeroplanes?

Deirdre They'll blend in. Stop fussing.

Tottie Where are we meant to be anyway?

Deirdre Messina. In Italy.

Tottie Right. (*Glancing around*) But where is everybody?

Deirdre (*standing up, pointing* R) Look look! The actors are coming. Here they come! (*Clapping excitedly*) Oh well done! Now we're off!

Tottie No, we're not. They're going back. I said I felt a spot of rain.

Deirdre (*crossly*) A spot won't melt them. Where are they going? Sugar babies!

Tottie Maybe that was the opening chorus.

Deirdre Don't be silly. They usually start with a tucket.

Tottie They never do!

Deirdre That means ...

Tottie I know what it means! Can't switch on the telly without seeing it right there in your room! Shouldn't be allowed! Squirming about with nothing on ...

Deirdre Do stop, Auntie! Oh dear, where have the actors gone off to now? One or two of them come a long way. Perhaps someone's late.

Tottie Who?

Deirdre I don't know. I'm just saying. Have another sandwich. I think you should put on some insect repellant. (*She takes a tube of cream from the basket*)

Tottie I don't think so!

Deirdre I don't mean on your sandwich! The mosquitos can get quite trying. They arrive at dusk, about half-time. Especially on a hot evening.

Tottie I'm not hot. I'm cold.

Deirdre Even so. People tend to put it on after they feel the first bite. Here, take it. (*She takes some cream and hands the tube to Tottie*)

Tottie (*taking the tube of cream reluctantly*) Lot of fuss!

Deirdre Put it on your wrists and ankles and forehead. Those are peaches and cream to a gnat.

Tottie Lot of bother!

Deirdre We had a terrible time on holiday in Africa with mosquitos near the river at sunset. They told us every fourth mosquito carried malaria. Robert used to count them. One, two, three — then go smack!

Tottie What a fool.

Deirdre It was a joke, Auntie.

Tottie Yes. It does sound like Robert.

Deirdre (*applying cream*) Anyway you'll be sorry to come out in lumps.

Tottie (*muttering*) It's all part of the fun, I suppose.

Deirdre You don't seem to be entering into the spirit of things.

Tottie I just wish they'd get going!

Deirdre They will! They will! (*Pointing*) There! I think they're getting into place right now. You'll really enjoy it, Auntie. When Beatrice and Benedick start in on each other they say the most insulting things.

Tottie Sounds like your Uncle Bert and Aunt Peggy!

Deirdre Not a bit! It's witty railery. And they're actually in love with each other, deep down.

Tottie You're right. Not a bit like Bert and Peggy.

Deirdre More like *When Harry Met Sally*.

Tottie Harry and Sally who?

Deirdre Never mind. Oh look! They're all behind that bush now. Put your specs on, Auntie. You don't want to miss their first entrance. Claudio was at school with Helen, you know.

Tottie Helen who? And who's Claudia? I wish you wouldn't keep talking about complete strangers.

Deirdre Claudio! Claudio! I don't think you read the synopsis at all.

Tottie It wasn't that easy to follow.

Deirdre Nonsense! The plot is simplicity itself. I'll explain. Beatrice and Benedick are always fighting each other. Scoring points. You understood that?

Tottie Yes.

Deirdre Beatrice is staying with her cousin Hero, who is the daughter of the Governor of Messina. Now, Hero is all set to marry Claudio, who is Benedick's best friend. Right? Meantime, everyone thinks it would be lots of fun if they contrived to make Benedick and Beatrice fall in love. So ... They arrange for them separately to overhear friends saying that each loves the other. And they both believe it. Because in fact, of course, they do.

Tottie Deep down.

Deirdre Although they hadn't realized it. So … Anyway a double wedding is planned. All right so far?

Tottie Well …

Deirdre Then there's a horrible plot to ruin the reputation of Hero.

Tottie Why would they do that?

Deirdre It's hatched by Don John. Don John is a very jealous of Claudio. He's a villianous man who is a bastard.

Tottie Sounds it.

Deirdre Don John tells Claudio that if he watches with him in the garden, he'll see Hero at her bedroom window talking to a strange man — the very night before the wedding! Claudio is persuaded to do it. And he believes he sees it happen. Although it's actually a maidservant whose been bribed to impersonate Hero.

Tottie Would you know!

Deirdre Next day — at the wedding — in the church — at the altar, Claudio denounces Hero as a strumpet.

Tottie A strumpet. Well that's not very nice.

Deirdre Hero faints with shock.

Tottie I'm not surprised. She's whiter than snow after all.

Deirdre Do listen, Auntie. Well, they all decide to tell Claudio that Hero's dead.

Tottie Serve him right.

Deirdre Beatrice tells Benedick that if he truly loves her he should avenge her cousin. And kill Claudio! Now, it's difficult for Benedick because Claudio is his best friend, of course. But Benedick agrees.

Tottie Good man.

Deirdre But in the nick of time they discover who carried out the plot.

Tottie Gave them a thumping, I hope.

Deirdre Of course. Prison — banishment — the lot.

Tottie Well done! Thank you, pet.

Deirdre Then they …

Tottie There's more?

Deirdre (*firmly*) So … then Hero's father arranges for Claudio to marry a girl who he says is Hero's cousin.

Tottie Is he mad?

Deirdre Although really it's Hero in a mask.

Tottie He *is* mad!

Deirdre You see Hero has forgiven Claudio for being taken in by Don John.

Tottie I wouldn't have.

Deirdre Well, Hero's still in love with him.

Tottie She'll regret it.

Deirdre Claudio turns up to marry the cousin and Hero takes off her mask.

Tottie It'll never work.

Deirdre Anyway, Claudio is delighted that Hero is alive after all.

Tottie It's all right for him. But mark my words, it's doomed from the start. Claudio's clearly a nitwit.

Deirdre (*crossly*) I don't think this play is really for you, Auntie. Shall we leave?

Tottie Oh no. What else would we do? I'm here for the weekend! (*Patting Deirdre's arm*) I'm having a great time, love.

Deirdre (*muttering*) And it's only Friday.

Tottie And I'm beginning to understand the play. The heroine is Hero.

Deirdre (*gritting her teeth*) Yes. She's Hero. OK?

Tottie Funny name though.

Deirdre Not at all. I suppose a writer can call his characters anything he likes. Why not?

Tottie Why not? Still it would have been easier all round if he'd called her Tracy.

Deirdre Why not Sharon! Those are modern names! Naturally, he uses Elizabethan names. She's called *Hero*, all right!

Tottie Beatrice is a modern name.

Deirdre No it's not!

Tottie My cousin was called Beatrice. Don't you remember your Auntie Beatie?

Deirdre No!

Tottie You must. She was a great one for the cruises. And one time going round the Mediterranean, she told me the purser —

Deirdre (*interrupting*) Don't you care about the plot! Don't you care if Beatrice and Benedick get married? And that each of them declares they're only marrying because the other won't survive if they don't. It's very funny. Don't you care?

Tottie Not a lot.

Deirdre *Well, I'm telling you!* Otherwise you won't enjoy it so much.

Tottie Won't I?

Deirdre No, you won't! You'll be quite lost!

Tottie Will I?

Deirdre Oh for heaven's sake! I give up! (*Grimly*) I really do think we'd better go! And I'll look up the time of your next train home!

Tottie No need to get like that.

Deirdre This is clearly a big mistake! Get up.

Tottie What?

Deirdre Get *up*!

Deirdre wrests the chair from under Tottie

Tottie You've got a very short fuse, you have. No wonder Robert spends his life on the golf course. (*She wanders* L)

Deirdre (*stopping dead*) What do you mean by that? Eh?
Tottie (*turning and pointing off* R) Deirdre, I think ——
Deirdre What are you saying about Robert? Eh?
Tottie Dierdre, someone's beckoning ——
Deirdre Don't change the subject. What do you mean about Robert.
   Eh?
Tottie Deirdre — over there — someone's waving at you.
Deirdre Never mind that. You just said something very provocative!
Tottie Everyone's beckoning and waving, Deirdre. Right over there!
   Look, look!
Deirdre What? (*Peering off* R) Oh my God!
Tottie What? What?
Deirdre Oh my God, would you believe it? They've set the scene up on
   the other lawn. They've never done that before. Ever!
Tottie Have we got to move?
Deirdre If we want to see the play — yes! Move! (*She frantically clears
   up during the following*) Move, Auntie! Oh botheration! Now where
   will we put our chairs!
Tottie Everyone's right over there.
Deirdre I know! Why didn't they tell us! Put the champagne back in
   the basket, Auntie.
Tottie We haven't got it open yet. I'll carry it.
Deirdre Quickly!

*There is the distant flourish of a trumpet, continuing under the
following*

Tottie I thought I heard a trumpet.
Deirdre A what? Oh, it's the tucket!
Tottie What?
Deirdre (*madly*) Tucket! Tucket!
Tottie Deirdre, I wish you wouldn't. Mind you, I do agree.
Deirdre (*calling* R *as she gathers her gear together*) We're coming!
   We're coming! Wait for us! Won't be long! (*Laden with all the gear,
   as at the beginning*) Have we got everything?
Tottie You've got everything, pet. Yes.
Deirdre Follow me, then! We'll find a place over there wherever we
   can. Probably right at the back! Hurry up, Auntie! Follow me! Follow
   me!

Deirdre staggers off R

Tottie watches Deirdre go until she is out of sight. Then she quietly tiptoes off L

The trumpet blows on as ——

—— *the* CURTAIN *falls*

REMEMBER ME

CHARACTERS

Elizabeth: 40/50
Sarah: 40/50

Scene — a quiet corner of a garden during a wedding reception
Time — the present

A quiet corner of a garden during a wedding reception

C *are two director's chairs facing out front with, between them, a small table. Two other garden chairs are set casually, one* R *and one* L

The CURTAIN *rises. The sounds of voices, laughter and snatches of a jazz band can be heard in the distance. These sounds get quieter as the dialogue gets going*

Sarah enters R. *She is an attractive woman between forty and fifty, dressed in a smart wedding-guest outfit with a hat and handbag. She is carrying a glass of champagne. She moves* DC, *thoughtfully*

Elizabeth (*off; in the distance, calling*) Sarah!

Sarah turns and looks off R, *frowning. She makes to leave* L

(*Her voice closer and louder; off*) Sarah!

Elizabeth enters R. *She is much the same age as Sarah, very attractive and wearing a stunning wedding-guest outfit with a hat and handbag, and several jangling bracelets on her wrist. She has a glass of champagne in one hand and a champagne bottle in the other*

(*Calling*) Sarah! Sarah!

Sarah pauses

Where are you tearing off to?

Sarah turns back. She regards Elizabeth steadily

That's better. I thought for moment I'd made a booboo and it wasn't you at all. But it certainly is! Oh yes! (*Pause*) We-ell? Come on! Remember me? (*Pause*) Remember me? Elizabeth!

Pause

Sarah (*nodding at last; quietly*) Yes. I remember you.

Elizabeth I should think so. (*She puts the bottle and her handbag on the table*)

Sarah It's a long time.

Elizabeth I can't have changed that much, can I? Oh, I know my hair's different.

Sarah It was down to your waist then.

Elizabeth So it was! (*She holds out her hand, thus displaying her bracelets*) Darling Sarah! It's delicious to see you. I'd no idea you'd be here. Might easily have missed each other among this avalanche of guests.

Sarah (*evenly*) Yes, we might. (*She does not take Elizabeth's hand*)

Elizabeth turns away, unfazed. She takes a drink and looks offstage R

Elizabeth God, they've pushed the boat out. Wedding of the year, my dear. Not difficult in this backwater. (*Turning back to Sarah*) You kept in touch with Jenny and Pete, then.

Sarah Christmas cards.

Elizabeth Me too. Quite surprised to get this invitation. They seem to have asked the whole uni lot. Neat. The two of them getting together. Losing their partners at the same time. Neat ending.

Sarah Happy ending, one hopes.

Elizabeth Hope springs eternal. (*Pause*) Did you marry?

Sarah Oh yes.

Elizabeth Me too. My husband is over there in the booze tent. Helping with Jenny's ancient aunt. She's drunk, I think. She was conducting the jazz band for a while. Then she started weeping. Then sobbing her heart out across a table. At that point a couple of chaps tried to heave her away. Her skinny old legs were dangling down like two pieces of spaghetti. Killing! My husband's probably settled her by now. Good at dealing with the drunk and disorderly, my husband. (*Pause. She looks at Sarah*) His name's Simon.

Sarah Ah.

Elizabeth Are you surprised? Did you think it would be — someone you knew?

Sarah No. I didn't think it would be. Not in a million years.

Elizabeth laughs. Pause

Elizabeth We should have kept in touch, Sarah.

Sarah You're incredible. You always were.

Elizabeth You take everything so seriously. You always did.

Sarah Not at all. That was the trouble. I didn't. And there were things I should have taken seriously. One thing anyway. But then I was young and innocent. It's a good state to be in, mind you. Believing the best of everyone. You never quite get back to it.

Elizabeth Like Oscar Wilde's peach. Touch it and the bloom is gone. (*She giggles*)

Sarah does not respond. There is a long pause. Elizabeth drinks. Sarah drinks. Both are busy with their own thoughts. Elizabeth looks at Sarah

You hadn't really forgotten me, had you?

Sarah How could I?

Elizabeth That's right. We did share that crummy flat after all, for how long was it? About ——

Sarah Two years.

Elizabeth Two years. (*Laughing*) What a learning curve.

Sarah It was for me.

Elizabeth You never forget the first girlfriend you share a place with. Nor your first boyfriend!

Sarah You had so many.

Elizabeth So did you.

Sarah Only one who mattered. (*Pause*) You remember who that was?

Elizabeth No. Why should I?

Sarah Oh, I think you should.

Elizabeth No idea. After all, it was your boyfriend.

Sarah Exactly.

Elizabeth Well, what was his name?

Sarah Oh, Elizabeth. (*Pause*) Huw, Huw from Wales. You remember him.

Elizabeth Huw?

Sarah Huw. Have the fine details faded? (*Lightly*) Someone brought him to a flat-warming party. Remember? Is it coming back? And I fell in love with him. But you know that. Just as you knew it then. That's right. You never ever forget your first love. Nor the person who takes him away from you.

Pause. Elizabeth looks away. She laughs awkwardly. She rubs her ankle during the following

Elizabeth You're getting maudlin. You've been guzzling the champagne. Me, I'm utterly footsore. New shoes are a great mistake worn at weddings. Too much standing around. There was a chair here. That's what I need.

Elizabeth staggers across R, *takes off her hat and puts it on a chair. She moves to the chair* R *of the table, sits and kicks off her shoes. Sarah moves round the back of the table and stands looking down at Elizabeth*

Sarah Strange. That's how I remember you. Always kicking off your shoes. Barefoot and sitting on the floor. You were sitting thus when I brought in the coffee.

Elizabeth What are you talking about?

Sarah At his feet ... You sat — gazing into his face.

Elizabeth Well, of course I was.

Sarah So you do remember.

Elizabeth No. It just seems obvious.

Sarah Of course it does. Your natural pose!

Elizabeth Oh Sarah! Jealousy. After all this time! Jealousy makes your face quite ugly.

Sarah You were never jealous in your life.

Elizabeth No, I don't think I was.

Sarah No. Not an emotion you'd ever experience. Why should you? You inspired it, though. Yes indeed. Quite a hobby.

Elizabeth That's not very nice.

Sarah I don't do "nice" so much these days. I don't get so easily fooled.

Elizabeth I don't think I'm enjoying this!

Sarah It was *you* who came across to *me*.

Elizabeth I was expecting a giggle over old times. Fat chance.

Sarah You opened up the can when you came over. They're all crawling out now — the recollections.

Elizabeth Did you have a thoroughly miserable life or what!

Sarah Not at all.

Elizabeth Well, then. Are you happily married?

Sarah Yes.

Elizabeth Very?

Sarah Yes, very.

Elizabeth Is he here?

Sarah (*after a pause*) Yes, he's here.

Elizabeth (*grinning*) It's not Huw, surely!

Sarah Of course not.

Elizabeth So why all the fuss about that wretched Welsh leek?

Sarah (*crossing* L) It's not just about Huw. (*Turning back*) It's just a chance to get answers.

Elizabeth Well don't interrogate me. You're the one with the instant recall. I've done a whole lot of interesting things since then. I don't think two years sharing life with you in Balham was one of them.The whole unrivetting episode is quite wiped from my mind.

Sarah I don't believe you. Anyway, it's an opportunity for me now. I'll try to remind you.

Elizabeth Please don't. Sit down and I'll top you up. (*She picks up the bottle, fills her own glass, the thrusts the bottle at Sarah*) Press on. I took it from a waiter.

Sarah refills her glass and drinks

(*Chattering*) God knows, Pete can afford it now. Being a director of you-know-who and all. Loaded or what! That's nine-tenths of his attraction. The other tenth is a well-kept secret between him and his personal fitness coach. But I won't tell if you won't.

Sarah puts her glass on the table and moves L. She takes off her hat and puts it, and her bag, on the chair L. She perches on the chair and looks across at Elizabeth

Elizabeth (*pointing off* R) Doesn't Jenny look precious in silver lamé? Like a herring.

Sarah (*after a pause*) You see, I could never understand why it happened. I could never understand why you did it. I've always wondered how you could. And suddenly today you were here. I saw you across the crowd. And I was going to keep out of your way. Then you came up to me. Looking glowing as you always did. Not a care. Not the tiniest scintilla of remorse.

Elizabeth "Scintilla"! Oh, Sarah! "Scintilla".

Sarah Not a hint of the past.

Elizabeth Why the melodrama? Life's moved on. Many years on, duckie! Why rake it up?

Sarah Because you're sitting here beside me. And I never expected to see you again. And I can't let the chance pass.

Elizabeth Well, I can! (*She rises swiftly, shoves on her shoes and grabs her bag*) I don't have to sit here, actually! I'm supposed to be merrymaking at the wedding! Where's my bloody hat? (*She finds it*) I don't have to stay here! (*She makes to leave*)

Sarah Hear me out, Elizabeth. You owe me that.

Elizabeth Oh go on. Go on then. (*She settles back in her seat and kicks her shoes off again*)

As Sarah tells the following story it becomes very intense and painful

Sarah (*sitting in the chair to the* L *of the table; quietly*) As I said, you never forget your first love.

Elizabeth Hormones raging.

Sarah No. That first experience of your heart being involved. (*Pause*) Mine overwhelmed me. I learnt for the first time how it can consume you. Utterly. Like a madness. The tyranny of timing. The bondage to the telephone.

Elizabeth Today you'd have a mobile. No problem!

Sarah I didn't even possess a watch. I carried my alarm clock around in a paper bag to judge to the second when he'd cross the precinct from one class to another. To catch a glimpse of him. To exchange a wave with him was to be transported, heart singing for the rest of the day. Till evening, when he might call.

Elizabeth What a juggins.

Sarah A complete juggins. And if we met at a friend's place, I'd wait agonized until he came to my side. Blissful when he stood close by. Pray he'd stay. And he did. We spent more and more time together. When he went home to visit his family, he'd write me letters — on mauve notepaper. Wild paper and envelopes he had made up himself in the art class. A joke between us. I told you, Elizabeth. Remember? The letters came often. Over the wild mountains and down to Balham. Where things followed a well-tried pattern. Like the wedding today. And I told you everything, Elizabeth, didn't I?

Elizabeth Did you?

Sarah You know it. You were full of advice in those early days. Your experience of course, was considerable. I confided in you a lot in those early days. But as it became more special, more intimate, I shared it with you less. It had become too precious. Then you went away to Spain for three months.

Elizabeth Oh yes that summer in Granada! It was heaven! I came back speaking very good Spanish.

Sarah You came back with your hair bleached flaxen.

Elizabeth I came back with a perfect accent.

Sarah You came back with your whole body tanned golden.

Elizabeth I came back with a language degree — of a sort!

Sarah I'd written to you regularly. Because you demanded it. And weren't we true friends? I told you how it was between Huw and me. You knew he had become the whole of my life. That my entire happiness was all bound up with him.

Elizabeth Oh, wring my withers, why don't you!

Sarah You knew. Because I'd told you. Yet you still did it. Why?

Elizabeth drinks

Elizabeth Sarah, you're really being a pain.

Sarah If you'll tell me. If you'll explain. I'm listening.

Sarah drinks. Pause. Elizabeth drinks. She looks at Sarah who is regarding her intently

Elizabeth (*looking across at Sarah's hat and pointing to it*) I like your hat ...
Sarah What?
Elizabeth I like your hat.
Sarah But ...
Elizabeth But nothing. I like your hat
Sarah Funny. You always used to add a proviso, as I recall.
Elizabeth A proviso ... ?
Sarah "I like your dress. But you're a bit fat for pink."
Elizabeth (*laughing*) I never said that.
Sarah Oh, yes you did.
Elizabeth You make me sound a complete shit. I was fond of you, Sarah.
Sarah I think you were. That's what made it all so strange. I need it to be sorted.
Elizabeth Well, I don't! It's over long ago. And I don't remember.
Sarah You will! On your second evening back from Spain, Huw came round to the flat. You greeted each other. Quite lightly. I went to make us coffee. When I came back — less than ten minutes later — there you were ... Shoes off, sitting at his feet, gazing up at him. Lips apart. Straining towards him with attention. Vibrant with attention.
Elizabeth Sarah ...
Sarah A story about his childhood. About falling from a donkey on the beach and what his mother had said to the donkeyman. A funny, tender story. An intimate story. A story he had never told to me.
Elizabeth I don't remember.
Sarah You laughed into his eyes at the end of it. And he reached his hand out to me — and took the mug of coffee I was offering — without looking away from your face.
Elizabeth It didn't mean anything.
Sarah Oh? It was soon after that when you began to lower your voice when you got certain telephone calls. Calls that were remarkably short. And others that I realized I'd interrupted when I arrived home suddenly.
Elizabeth Sarah ...
Sarah I'd hear the receiver replaced as I pushed open the door. And I remember the nights when Huw was tied up with work and couldn't see me. Nights when you just happened to have a heavy date with someone you'd never mentioned before.

Elizabeth (*smiling slowly*) You were pretty dim, you know, weren't you?

Sarah Oh yes. Dim as they come, if you like. But it was more that I couldn't conceive it was happening. You were my best friend, weren't you? Huw was my lover. I couldn't imagine either of you hurting me — or not loving me in your different ways — as I loved you.

Elizabeth Stuff happens.

Sarah Everything I did, Huw was part of. I couldn't imagine a future that didn't include him. Even when he began to call me less often. Even when those whispered calls of yours got more frequent. (*Pause*) Then came that Christmas holiday. We'd had such plans. But he went to visit his parents for a fortnight. And he didn't come back. His letters arrived. The mauve letters. Easy to spot among the invitations and the bills. Then they too came less often. His father was ill and his mother needed him. I told him not to worry. Not to feel guilty if he couldn't write.

Elizabeth Honestly, Sarah ...

Sarah It's called trust, Elizabeth. Misplaced, of course. The letters got shorter — less ardent — more informative about the weather. The loving part was so — carefully phrased. Such a terrible politeness. Had someone else come into his life? It became a bewildering possibility. Then a shattering probability. It was the mauve envelope that finally did it.

Elizabeth You were certainly blinkered. (*She rises and moves* R)

Sarah No credit to you. The trusting are easy to fool. But I truly didn't realize it. Until the day the mauve envelope wasn't addressed to me but to you. (*Pause*) It wasn't very brave of Huw to do it that way. But it made his point. (*She rises and crosses to Elizabeth*) You picked it up with no attempt to hide it. You picked it up right under my nose. I got the message.

Elizabeth (*turning away*) What else was there to do?

Sarah And you gave a little shrug.

Elizabeth (*irritated*) Tch!

Sarah I'll remember that little shrug to my dying day, Elizabeth.

Elizabeth For heaven's sake! The booze is getting to both of us. Let's give it a rest.

Sarah If it was today I would stay and fight

Elizabeth (*mockingly*) Oh dear. I'm shaking.

Sarah Stay and fight you for the slimebag.

Elizabeth (*laughing*) Now that really would have been fun!

Sarah Fun? For whom?

Elizabeth Huw for one!

Sarah What?

Elizabeth A man likes to be fought for. Who doesn't?

Sarah Ah. I see. Maybe you're right.

Elizabeth I am right. I know the game backwards, Sarah.

Sarah Game? I never was any good at competitive sports.

Elizabeth No, you weren't.

Sarah Never liked them. Even less if it's one where the ball enjoys it more than the players.

Elizabeth It all depends how much you want the ball.

Sarah I suppose I'd have liked the ball to have a will of its own.

Elizabeth No chance!

Sarah I certainly found that out.

Elizabeth You lacked the killer instinct, darling.

Sarah (*closing in*) That was then.

Sarah slowly and firmly treads on Elizabeth's foot

Elizabeth (*gasping with pain*) What the hell are you doing? Get off my foot!

Sarah You'd be surprised how many times in those first years I dreamed of hitting you in the face. Could do it now really.

Elizabeth For God's sake, we're at a wedding!

Sarah Always emotional events, aren't they? (*She leans harder*)

Elizabeth Get off! Oh, God, my foot!

Sarah Shouldn't have taken your shoes off!

Elizabeth screams with pain. Sarah releases her foot

Never too late to bat an old friend. (*She hits Elizabeth's shoulder with the flat of her hand*)

Elizabeth retreats. Sarah pursues her and repeats the blow — quite sharply

Elizabeth (*gasping*) Stop it! You're hurting me.

Sarah Good.

Sarah drives Elizabeth to the chair R of the table. Elizabeth sits, cowering back. Sarah leans down over her very slowly, then suddenly claps her hands fiercely in her face

Elizabeth (*crying out*) You're mad!

Sarah picks up Elizabeth's hat. For a moment we think she might be about to destroy it. But she just throws it aside

(*Diving after the hat*) Do you mind! That cost money!
Sarah Well, I didn't think you knitted it.
Elizabeth Fool.

Pause. Elizabeth sits back in her seat. The tension has lessened. Elizabeth refills her glass. The bottle is empty now. Sarah sits L *of the table*

Sarah We need another bottle.
Elizabeth *You* don't. I didn't remember you being a drinker.
Sarah I'm not.
Elizabeth Maybe that was your problem. Never lightened up enough.
Sarah I never had a problem before *you*. Nor after you, for that matter.
Elizabeth Do you hate me so much?
Sarah Depends. Am I to get my answer?
Elizabeth I don't think you are. I don't know what to say. It just couldn't be helped.
Sarah But I know you didn't fall in love with him.
Elizabeth (*quietly*) No.
Sarah Have you ever? Could you ever?

Pause

Elizabeth (*brightly*) Come and meet my husband now! He'd like to meet someone who knew me of old.
Sarah Well, I certainly do that.
Elizabeth Do what?
Sarah Know you of old. Though I did my best to forget.
Elizabeth I told him I'd shared a flat once. He was surprised we never kept in touch. (*Pause*) You didn't need to move out like that, you know.
Sarah You're joking.
Elizabeth He wondered why I never saw you again. Thought it odd.
Sarah I never saw Huw again either.

Pause. The sound of guests' voices and laughter rises in the distance, fading again during the following

Elizabeth (*looking off* R) I believe the bride and groom are leaving. Must wave them off, I suppose.(*She picks up her bag, takes out lipstick and mirror and makes repairs*)

Sarah rises, moves L, *puts on her hat and picks up her bag. Elizabeth puts on her hat*

(*Licking her lips*) I'd adore to meet your husband, Sarah.

Sarah I don't think that's necessary.

Elizabeth Why not? (*With a slow, teasing smile*) Scared.

Sarah I don't scare so easily these days.

Elizabeth Well, then ... (*Rising*) Let's go and find him. What does he look like? Tall, good-looking, charming, devoted to his little wifey. Sexy?

Sarah All of those things.

Elizabeth I can't wait! I'm dying to get to know him. I bet he and Simon will get on famously. Tell you what — when this tiresome farce is over, we could all go on somewhere.

Sarah I pointed you out to him in the church. He knows you already.

Elizabeth He doesn't.

Sarah By reputation.

Elizabeth What?

Sarah He said to me, and I quote, "Say hello to the woman if you like. But please, Sarah, don't suggest we go on somewhere."

Elizabeth I don't follow. I've never met your cheesy husband in my life! I don't know him.

Sarah When I mentioned your name, he said he already knew you. He said that you were the reason his sister's husband left her. The woman who broke up the marriage. Then dumped him. I recognized the pattern, of course. Just for the hell of it, eh Elizabeth? Like always. (*Pause*) I suppose that's my answer when it comes down to it. You did it to prove you could.

Elizabeth And you believed him!

Sarah Ah ah! Don't start that one, Elizabeth. He said to me, "That woman is — "

Elizabeth What? Is what? What did he say!

Sarah Just one word.

Elizabeth One word?

Sarah But the right one. If he'd said the wrong one — "She's a ballbreaker" or something I might have thought it was just pub gossip. If he'd said a whole lot I might have suspected he'd known you personally — intimately. But no. He summed you up exactly, Elizabeth. He's wise, my husband. You can come over and I'll introduce you, but I'm not sure you'll enjoy it. You see, he got you in one. He said — you're — "unkind".

Elizabeth Unkind?

Sarah It's the perfect description of you. Everyone would agree. Live with it, Elizabeth.

Pause. The crowd noises swell up again

Time to throw some confetti. Well, shall I take you over to meet him?
Mm? But if I say "Here is my husband" please don't mistake it for a
gift. Because it isn't.
Elizabeth I don't think I'll bother.
Sarah Wise decision.

The two women regard each other levelly

Goodbye, Elizabeth. We won't meet again.
Elizabeth I hope not! (*She rubs her shoulder pointedly*) I'll remember
you, Sarah.

*Elizabeth takes a bag of confetti from her bag, takes a last look at
Sarah, then marches off* R

Sarah *watches her go and stands a moment in thought*

Sarah I won't count on it.

Sarah follows Elizabeth off R

The crowd noise swells up as —

— *the* CURTAIN *falls*

FURNITURE AND PROPERTY LIST

GARDEN PESTS

On stage: Two director's chairs

Off stage: Long umbrella, folded, holding about six shrub cuttings (**Helena**)
Long umbrella, folded, similar to **Helena**'s holding about twelve shrub cuttings (**Cath**)

Personal: **Helena**: Small handbag containing stylish foldaway raincoat; notepad, pen
Cath: Small handbag containing plastic-wrapped tuna sandwich, wrapped sweet, tube of insect-bite cream, white plastic coverall; notepad, pen

GRANNIES

On stage: Two municipal canvas chairs
Modern carrycot pram
Crime novel for **Jenny**

Off stage: Carriage-built pram containing life-like doll wearing pink bonnet and shawl (**Barbara**)

OUTDOOR PLEASURES

Off stage: Two director's chairs; picnic basket containing bottle of champagne, box of sandwiches, cartons of fruit juice; rug (**Deirdre**)
Umbrella (**Tottie**)

REMEMBER ME

On stage: Two director's chairs
Two other garden chairs

Off stage: Glass of champagne (**Sarah**)
Champagne bottle and glass of champagne (**Elizabeth**)

Personal: **Sarah**: handbag
Elizabeth: handbag containing lipstick, mirror and bag of confetti

LIGHTING PLOT

Garden Pests

To open: General bright exterior lighting. Dim slowly throughout play

No cues

Grannies

To open: General bright exterior lighting

No cues

Outdoor Pleasures

To open: General early summer evening light

No cues

Remember Me

To open: General exterior lighting

No cues

EFFECTS PLOT

GARDEN PESTS

Cue 1   **Helena**: "Better get back to the coaches."   (Page 12)
Sound of rain (continuous)

Cue 2   **Helena**: "Enough! Please! If you don't mind!"   (Page 13)
Sound of rain gets heavier. Thunder

Cue 3   **Helena** and **Cath** exit   (Page 13)
Increase storm sounds

GRANNIES

No cues

OUTDOOR PLEASURES

Cue 4   **Deirdre**: "Quickly!"   (Page 40)
Distant flourish of a trumpet; continuous

REMEMBER ME

Cue 5   When the CURTAIN rises   (Page 45)
Distant sounds of voices, laughter,
snatches of jazz band; continuous

Cue 6   **Sarah**: "I never saw Huw again either." Pause   (Page 54)
Sounds of voices, laughter,
fading under following action

Cue 7   **Sarah**: "Live with it, Elizabeth." Pause   (Page 55)
Crowd noises increase in volume

Cue 8   **Sarah** follows **Elizabeth** off   (Page 56)
Crowd noise swells